· VOICES ·
from
COLONIAL AMERICA

NEW FRANCE

1534 — 1763

FEATURING THE REGION THAT NOW INCLUDES ALL OR PARTS OF
MICHIGAN, MINNESOTA, WISCONSIN, ILLINOIS, INDIANA, OHIO,
PENNSYLVANIA, VERMONT, MAINE, AND
CANADA FROM MANITOBA TO NEWFOUNDLAND

RICHARD WORTH

WITH

JOSÉ ANTÓNIO BRANDÃO, PH.D., CONSULTANT

NATIONAL GEOGRAPHIC

WASHINGTON, D.C.

John M. Fahey, Jr., *President and Chief Executive Officer*
Gilbert M. Grosvenor, *Chairman of the Board*
Nina D. Hoffman, *Executive Vice President; President, Book Publishing Group*

STAFF FOR THIS BOOK

Nancy Laties Feresten, *Vice President, Editor-in-Chief of Children's Books*
Amy Shields, *Executive Editor, Children's Books*
Suzanne Patrick Fonda, *Project Editor*
Robert D. Johnston, Ph.D., *Associate Professor and Director, Teaching of History Program University of Illinois at Chicago, Series Editor*
Bea Jackson, *Director of Illustration and Design, Children's Books*
Jean Cantu, *Illustrations Specialist*
Carl Mehler, *Director of Maps*
Justin Morrill, *The M Factory, Inc., Map Research, Design, and Production*
Rebecca Baines, *Editorial Assistant*
Jennifer Thornton, *Managing Editor*
Connie D. Binder, *Indexer*
R. Gary Colbert, *Production Director*
Lewis R. Bassford, *Production Manager*
Nicole Elliott and Maryclare Tracy, *Manufacturing Managers*

Voices from Colonial Maryland was prepared by
CREATIVE MEDIA APPLICATIONS, INC.

Richard Worth, *Writer*
Fabia Wargin Design, Inc., *Design and Production*
Susan Madoff, *Editor*
Laurie Lieb, *Copyeditor*
Cynthia Joyce, *Image Researcher*

Body text is set in Deepdene, sidebars are Caslon 337 Oldstyle, and display text is Cochin Archaic Bold.

LIBRARY OF CONGRESS CATALOGING-IN-PUBLICATION DATA
Worth, Richard.
   Voices from colonial America : New France 1534–1763 : featuring the region that now includes all or parts of Michigan, Minnesota, Wisconsin, Illinois, Indiana, Ohio, Pennsylvania, Vermont, Maine, and Canada from Manitoba to Newfoundland / by Richard Worth.
      p. cm. — (Voices from colonial America)
      Includes bibliographical references and index.
   ISBN 978-1-4263-0147-6 (hardcover, trade : alk. paper) —
   ISBN 978-1-4263-0148-3 (hardcover, library : alk. paper)
1. Canada—History—To 1763 (New France)—Juvenile literature. 2. French—North America—History—Juvenile literature. 3. North America—History—Colonial period, ca. 1600–1775—Juvenile literature. I. Title.
   F1030.W67 2007
   971.01'8—dc22
                                        2007029544
Printed in the United States

CONTENTS

New France

1 7 1 9

CARTE DE LA NOUVELLE FRANCE, où ... RENS & de MISSISSIPI Aujour d'hui S. LO

Aux Environs des-quelles se trouvent les ETATS, PAIS, NATIO ... de la VIRGINIE, de la MARIE-LANDE, de la PENSIL

du NOUVEAU JERSAY, de la NOUVELLE YORCK, de la NOUV. ANGLETERRE, de L'ACADIE, du CANADA, des ESQUIMAUX, des HURONS, des IROQUOIS, des ILINOIS &

Grande Ile de TERRE NEUVE: Dressée sur les MEMOIRES lès plus NOUVEAUX, recueillis pour L'ETABLISSEMENT de la COMPAGNIE FRANÇOISE OCCID

Area of New France shown in red on the 1719 historical map

Area of New France in 1719 according to modern historians

INTRODUCTION

by

José António Brandão, Ph.D.

Inhabitants of New France travel to and from Québec (seen in
background) over the frozen St. Lawrence in horse-drawn sleighs.

Looking at the United States of America today, it is often
hard to imagine that it was once a collection of European-
controlled colonies, each struggling to survive. But the history of North America, in general, and the United States in
particular, is a story of struggle by colonists of different
cultural backgrounds for control of land, resources, and

OPPOSITE: This historic map highlights in red areas of New France that
were the main regions of exploration or settlement in the early 1700s.
The inset map shows the present-day provinces and states that
made up this area.

their own existence. The country was shaped by this struggle with native peoples, Spaniards, Swedes, the Dutch, the English, and the focus of this volume: French settlers in Nouvelle France (New France in English).

Once, large portions of what is now the United States were claimed by a French monarchy and settled by French-speaking peoples. With a population a fraction of that of the 13 Colonies, the French managed to explore, map, and claim much of the interior of the continent, including the St. Lawrence River valley, the Great Lakes, and the Mississippi and Ohio river systems. They also succeeded in keeping English-speaking settlement largely confined to the region east of the Appalachian Mountains.

The French were able to contain the English, in part, because of their strategic location along the major water routes into the interior of North America and due to the fur trade. The latter allowed them to establish trade and military alliances with native peoples in the Great Lakes and Mississippi watersheds. Those alliances were crucial in helping the small French population explore and settle in new lands and in keeping other Europeans away. For the Indians, the alliances with the French gave them access to new goods and technologies that allowed them to pursue their own strategic goals, which included defeating old enemies and protecting their lands from other Indians and from Europeans.

It was only after the French and their Indian allies were defeated and were no longer a military threat, that the 13 Colonies were truly secure and settlers from those places could begin the slow march west that eventually led to the creation of the United States we now know. And today Americans, especially those who live in areas once settled by the French, need only pay a little attention to see what remains of that contest for North America. French place-names for rivers, lakes, cities, and even a state (Louisiana), mark the legacy of New France and reveal how central the contest for North America was in shaping the United States.

I am pleased to serve as consultant for *Voices from Colonial America: New France*, which seeks to broaden the understanding of colonial America by including different voices in telling young Americans the story of their colonial past.

A drawing of a *coureur de bois* by Frederic Remington

CHAPTER ONE

The Founding of New France

French explorers attempt to colonize Canada in North America in the 16th-century. Success will not come until Samuel de Champlain settles the region six decades later.

 rench explorations in North America that led to the founding of New France began during the early 1500s.

Jacques Cartier, a master seaman from Saint-Malo on the coast of France, led some of the most important early voyages to North America. On his first voyage, Cartier left

OPPOSITE: Jacques Cartier and his party of explorers travel up the St. Lawrence River in 1535.

from Saint-Malo with two sailing ships and 61 men in 1534. The French explorer hoped to find a route to the Orient by sailing west. The lands in the East were rich in spices that French merchants hoped to sell in Europe. Cartier thought that there might be a water passage through North America that would take him to Asia.

French fishing fleets were already operating off the coast of North America. They caught large quantities of cod. The fish was salted to preserve it, then taken back to Europe, where it found a ready market. Most Europeans were Roman Catholics, and the Catholic Church required its members to eat only fish, not meat, about 150 days each year.

During his first voyage, Cartier explored Labrador and Newfoundland off the coast of present-day Canada. He also entered the mouth of the St. Lawrence River. This long river flows for more than 700 miles (1,130 km) from the Atlantic Ocean to Lake Ontario, the easternmost of the Great Lakes. Along the way, Cartier met a group of natives. They *"set up a great clamor and made frequent signs to us to come on shore, holding up to us some furs on sticks."* Cartier traded trinkets for furs. Beaver fur was in great demand in Europe to make fashionable hats and coats for the wealthy. After meeting with the Indians, Cartier returned to France.

The following year, Cartier went back to North America. This time, he sailed with three ships and about 110 men westward along the St. Lawrence River. Cartier hoped that the river might provide a water route to China.

"This river," said Cartier, "flows between high mountains of bare rock, which nevertheless support a vast quantity of trees of various kinds . . . we saw a tree suitable for masting a ship of 30 tons, and as green as it could be, growing out of a rock without a trace of earth."

French seaman Jacques Cartier

Accompanying Cartier on this trip were several Indians, whom he had captured on his first visit to North America. Two of them, Domagaya and Taignoagny, acted as his guides. They took him to a village called Stadacona along the river. When he asked the Indians where he was, the Indians answered *Kanata*. Cartier thought this was the name of the region, but it really means "village." Cartier named the waterway the River of Canada. Later the name was changed to the St. Lawrence—the name of a Christian saint—but Canada became the name of the land. Stadacona lay under a large rocky cliff and had a commanding view of the St. Lawrence River. This rocky area became the future site of the city of Québec.

As Cartier continued westward along the river, he reached a village called Hochelaga, which was protected by wooden walls and surrounded by fields of corn.

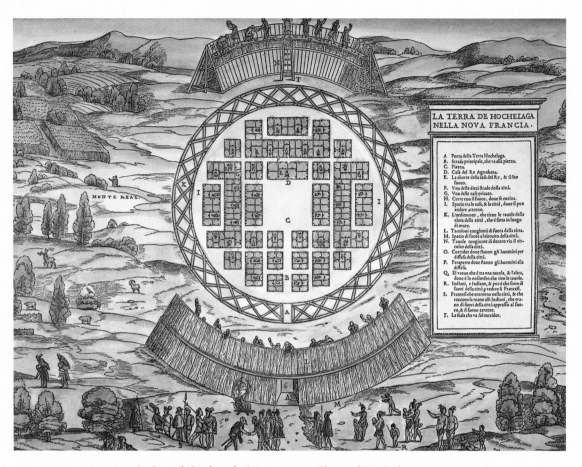

A printed plan of the fortified Iroquoian village of Hochelaga near present-day Montréal shows Jacques Cartier being greeted by the Indians. He named the elevated area in the background Mont Royal. The image comes from the book *Delle navigationi et viaggi* (*Some Voyages and Travels*), by Italian geographer Giovanni Battista Ramusio, published in the late 1500s.

Overlooking Hochelaga was a high hill that Cartier called Mont Royal—the future site of Montréal. Then Cartier and his men returned to Stadacona, where they spent the winter. The river had frozen over, making it impossible for them to leave. The French explorers battled heavy snows and howling winds. Many of them died before Cartier could finally return to France the following spring. He kidnapped several natives and took them with him as hostages until he returned to America. This was his way of ensuring the loyalty of the Indians in Canada. But Cartier did not come back to the region until 1541. This time he encountered hostile Indians, so he decided to abandon his plans for new explorations. In 1542, he went back to France. The French had tried to establish a foothold in Canada, but failed. As a result of this failure, they abandoned their exploration efforts for 60 years.

THE COLONY OF NEW FRANCE

The voyages of Jacques Cartier would inspire more exploration and the founding of New France, a French colony that eventually stretched from Newfoundland westward to Lake Superior. The colony also included a vast region called Louisiana, which stretched from the Appalachians to the Rockies and south to the Gulf of Mexico. (This region is explored in *Voices from Colonial America: Louisiana.*) New France covered several provinces of present-day Canada, including Newfoundland and Labrador, Nova Scotia, New Brunswick, Prince Edward Island, Québec, Ontario, and Manitoba. French settlements, posts, and missions were also established in the current states of Maine, Vermont, New York, Michigan,

Wisconsin, and Minnesota, and in Illinois Country. Finally, the French claimed the Ohio River Valley, made up of western Pennsylvania and Ohio—a territory that was also claimed by England.

A hand-colored woodcut of Niagara Falls illustrates the abundance of beavers in the region in the 17th and early 18th centuries by exaggerating the number of animals seen at work along the river. In addition to beaver pelts, New France exported large quantities of fur and hides from bears, deer, otters, foxes, mink, and moose.

New France became a valuable part of the French Empire thanks to a plentiful supply of beaver and the high prices its fur commanded in Europe. In order to gain a strong footing in the fur trade, France, through the years,

Huguenots—French
Protestants

attempted to establish a presence in North America from several directions. French Huguenots established Fort Caroline, a settlement along the Atlantic coast in present-day Jacksonville, Florida, but their colony was destroyed by the Spanish in 1564. Subsequent attempts down the St. Lawrence River and through the Mississippi Valley proved more successful. The search for beaver also led the colonists of New France into alliances with Indian nations, which supplied most of the pelts. The French established forts to cement these alliances and protect the fur trade.

French fur trade, French forts, and French alliances—these formed the foundation of the colony of New France.

CHAMPLAIN ESTABLISHES NEW FRANCE

In the last decades of the 16th century, French fishermen continued to catch cod off the coast of Canada. They also traded for beaver fur. Small settlements sprang up where fishermen dried their cod and defended their fishing grounds. In 1600, the French tried to establish a permanent settlement at Tadoussac, a fur trading post on the St. Lawrence River. But the harsh Canadian winter took the lives of most of the settlers.

Meanwhile, the French king Henri IV had granted the right to control the fur trade to Vice Admiral Aymar de

ACADIA

IN 1611, CHARLES DE BIENCOURT LED A SECOND EXPEDITION to Port Royal. He was the son of sieur de Poutrincourt, one of the men who had sailed with sieur de Monts and Champlain in 1604. No women accompanied the expedition to help in the fields, and the settlement struggled. Shortly afterward, Port Royal was attacked by the English, who believed they had a claim to the region. They burned all the houses while the French settlers were out in their fields, several miles away. The settlers recovered, built new homes, and eventually received supplies from France.

Meanwhile, ownership of Acadia was disputed between the French and the English. The English king James I awarded it to one of his supporters, the Count of Sterling, in 1621. Few settled there, and the territory was turned over to France in 1632.

During the next decades, the French established settlements at La Hève, Cape Sable, and St. Ann. A census in 1671 showed 392 people in Acadia, most of them living in Port Royal. The population reached 1,700 by the beginning of the next century. François-Marie Perrot, the commander of Acadia during the 1680s, described the *"simple, pastoral existence"* of the Acadians: *"They lived better than Canadians [French settlers in other regions of New France] for they never lacked bread or meat. But they weren't as industrious, and never put away harvests in case of a bad year."*

The founding of Québec by Samuel de Champlain in 1608 established the French foothold in North America. His group of about 28 explorers spent the winter in New France. Nineteen died, but Champlain did not abandon his attempt to establish a settlement. As he put it, he wanted *"to lay the foundation of a permanent edifice, as well for the glory of God as for the renown of the French."* In the spring, a ship arrived with more men and supplies. Champlain decided to travel west along the river to begin trading for fur with the local Indians.

This 1632 map drawn by Champlain shows New France and neighboring regions. The map also indicates where various Indian nations lived and the many water routes that acted as highways for the fur trade that provided the foundation of New France's economy.

CHAPTER TWO

Native Peoples of New France

FRANCE FORMS ALLIANCES *with native groups in New France in order to build a thriving fur trade.*

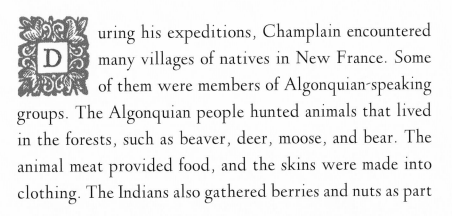 uring his expeditions, Champlain encountered many villages of natives in New France. Some of them were members of Algonquian-speaking groups. The Algonquian people hunted animals that lived in the forests, such as beaver, deer, moose, and bear. The animal meat provided food, and the skins were made into clothing. The Indians also gathered berries and nuts as part

OPPOSITE: A portrait of Tee Yee Ho Ga Row, one of four chiefs of the Five Nations of the Iroquois Confederacy who traveled to London in 1710. At his feet are a wolf and a tomahawk, which symbolize strength and courage of the chief's clan. Tee Yee Ho Ga Row is holding a wampum belt used in, among other ways, diplomatic encounters between Indians and Indians, and Indians and Europeans.

of their diet. Several Algonquian families lived together as a band in a single village. Each village was governed by a sachem, or chief. The villages included teepees made of birchbark, stripped from nearby trees. The Algonquians also used birch trees to make canoes that they used to travel along the rivers and fish for food. Among those Algonquian speakers who became important allies of the French were the Petite Nation and the Kichesipirini, whom the French called the Ottawa River Algonquins. Other important Algonquian-speaking allies included the Potawatomi, Ottawa, and Ojibwa nations of the upper Great Lakes region.

In addition to the Algonquians, another large group of native peoples belonged to the Iroquoian language family. As many as 90,000 natives who were part of the Iroquoian language family lived in what is now Canada in 1600. Among them were the Hurons, who lived in present-day southern Ontario. Other Iroquoian speakers lived south of Lake Ontario. These included the Senecas, Cayugas, Onondagas, Oneidas, and Mohawks, who together formed the League of the Five Nations of Iroquois. (Although the Hurons were speakers of the Iroquoian language, they were not members of the Five Nations of Iroquois.) Chiefs from the Five Nations met together regularly to make major decisions, such as whether to go to war. This alliance of the Five Nations meant that they could put a large number of warriors into battle to defend their lands. The homelands of the Five Nations stretched from the Genesee River in what is western New York State to the Hudson River and Lake Champlain in the east.

Each spring, Indians in New France tapped maple trees and then boiled the sap in order to make maple sugar, an important ingredient in many of the foods they prepared. This method, taught to the early settlers of New France, is still used to make maple sugar and maple syrup.

The Iroquoian-speaking groups not only hunted like the Algonquians, they also cultivated food in large communal fields. These fields, which surrounded their villages, were maintained by the Iroquoian women. They grew corn, beans, squash, and tobacco. Villages consisted of long-houses made of wood covered in bark. A group of Iroquoian families lived together in houses that might be 60 yards long and 12 yards wide. Each village was surrounded by a wooden stockade that provided defense against their ene-mies. Warfare broke out regularly between the Five Nations and the Hurons or between Iroquoian speakers and Algonquian speakers. Wars were fought to seek revenge for past attacks, take captives, and protect their territory.

CHAMPLAIN AND THE NATIVE PEOPLES

The Hurons and Algonquians were a better source for furs than the Iroquois so Champlain supported them in their wars against the Five Nations. In 1609, he and some of his men accompanied a war party of Hurons in a raid against their Iroquois enemies. The expedition traveled southward from the St. Lawrence River to a large lake. Champlain named it after himself—Lake Champlain.

The raiding party camped for the night in the forest not far from an Iroquois village. Champlain wrote that he had a dream in which he saw the Iroquois drowning in a lake. When he told his native allies about the dream the next morning, it *"gave them so much confidence that they did not doubt any longer that good was to happen to them."* As it turned out, Champlain's dream proved correct. When the war party advanced into battle, Champlain and his men led the attack. They carried arquebuses against the Iroquois' bows and arrows. *"I rested my musket against my cheek,"* Champlain wrote, *"and aimed*

arquebus—a 15th-century musket

directly at one of the three chiefs. With the same shot, two fell to the ground; and one of their men was so wounded that he died some time after. I had loaded my musket with four balls. . . . This caused great alarm among them. As I was loading again, one of my companions fired a shot from the woods, which astonished them anew to such a degree that, seeing their chiefs dead, they lost courage, and took flight."

In 1610, Samuel de Champlain, allied with Algonquians and Hurons, fought the Iroquois along the Richelieu River by attacking a fortified encampment. Champlain engaged in a number of these battles against the Iroquois, who tried to interfere with New France's fur trade with the Algonquians and Hurons.

This was not Champlain's only successful expedition against the Iroquois. A similar fight in 1610 also ended in defeat for the Iroquois. These early battles laid the foundation of a close relationship between the French and their Indian allies.

ÉTIENNE BRULÉ
and the
COUREURS DE BOIS

AS PART OF HIS EFFORT TO PROMOTE THE FUR TRADE, Champlain sent out French settlers to live among the Indians. They were called *coureurs de bois*—runners of the woods. One of these men was Étienne Brulé, a friend of Champlain. Born in the early 1590s in France, Brulé may have accompanied Champlain to New France in 1608. Beginning in 1610, he spent five years among the Hurons, learning their language and developing close relationships with these Indians. He also explored various parts of New France. As Champlain said, *"I had with me a youth who had already spent two winters at Québec and wanted to go among the [Indians] to master their language . . . learn their country . . . take note of the rivers and the peoples living along them."*

In 1615, Champlain went west and visited with Brulé on Lake Huron. He then directed Brulé to continue his explorations southward. With Huron scouts to lead him, Brulé traveled to present-day Buffalo, New York. During the following spring, he was captured by the Iroquois. He managed to save his life by promising *"to bring them into agreement with the French, & their foes, & to make them swear friendship with one another."* Brulé's explorations continued over the next decade. He returned to the Hurons where he was eventually killed and eaten by the Indians he had lived among.

CHAMPLAIN'S EXPEDITIONS

Over the next decade, Champlain continued to promote the fur trade and French alliances with the Indian nations. In 1615, he traveled along the Ottawa River and spent about a month among the Hurons, learning more about their way of life. He also recognized the power of the Huron Confederacy. This was an alliance of several Native American groups, numbering more than 30,000 Indians. The Hurons brought furs from the Indian groups farther west and traded them with the French. Later that year, Champlain joined another raiding party against the Iroquois. But this time the Iroquois defeated the French and their allies, wounding Champlain. He was nursed back to health by the Hurons.

Meanwhile, Champlain was trying to convince the French government to invest more money in New France. He also wanted the government to send out additional settlers to build homes in the new colony. During the late 1620s, Cardinal Richelieu, the chief minister of King Louis XIII, formed the Compagnie des Cent-Associés (Company of One Hundred Associates), an investment company of well-to-do French citizens. Their money paid for 400 settlers to travel to New France in 1628.

Champlain, appointed governor of New France by the Company of One Hundred Associates, recognized the importance of building larger settlements. These settlements

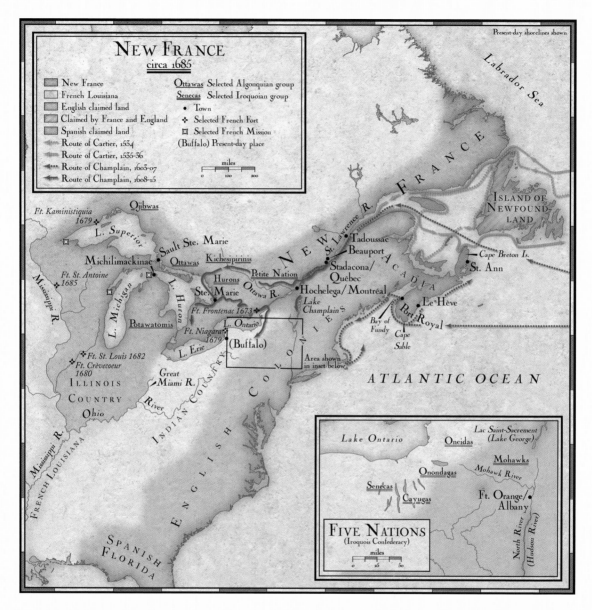

Present-day shorelines shown

New France
circa 1685

New France
French Louisiana
English claimed land
Claimed by France and England
Spanish claimed land
Route of Cartier, 1534
Route of Cartier, 1535-36
Route of Champlain, 1603-07
Route of Champlain, 1608-15

Ottawas   Selected Algonquian group
Senecas   Selected Iroquoian group
• Town
✦ Selected French Fort
☐ Selected French Mission
(Buffalo) Present-day place

miles
0   100   200

Labrador Sea

ISLAND OF NEWFOUND-LAND

N E W   F R A N C E

A C A D I A

Ojibwas
Ft. Kaministiquia 1679
L. Superior
Michilimackinac
Sault Ste. Marie
Ottawas
Kichesipirinis
Petite Nation
Ft. St. Antoine 1685
L. Michigan
L. Huron
Hurons
Ste. Marie
Ottawa R.
Potawatomis
Ft. Frontenac 1673
L. Ontario
Ft. Niagara 1679
(Buffalo)
L. Erie
Ft. St. Louis 1682
Ft. Crèvecoeur 1680
Great Miami R.
ILLINOIS COUNTRY
Ohio
Mississippi R.
INDIAN COUNTRY
River
FRENCH LOUISIANA
E N G L I S H   C O L O N I E S
SPANISH FLORIDA

St. Lawrence R.
Tadoussac
Beauport
Stadacona/Québec
Hochelega/Montréal
Lake Champlain
Le Hève
Port Royal
Bay of Fundy
Cape Sable
Cape Breton Is.
St. Ann

Area shown in inset below

A T L A N T I C   O C E A N

Five Nations
(Iroquois Confederacy)

Lake Ontario
Oneidas
Lac Saint-Sacrement (Lake George)
Onondagas
Mohawks
Mohawk River
Senecas
Cayugas
Ft. Orange/Albany
North River (Hudson River)

miles
0   25   50

By the end of the 1600s, Québec and Montréal had become the cultural and economic centers of New France, with settlement concentrated on farmland along the St. Lawrence River and in Acadia. Missions and forts, which protected the colony's fur trade, were operating around the Great Lakes and south to what came to be known as Illinois Country. Although the explorer La Salle claimed Louisiana (the Mississippi River and all land drained by it) for France in 1682, the French considered the land in the Ohio Valley and east of the Mississippi Indian Country. Keenly aware that people living in England's colonies outnumbered them, the French relied on alliances with native groups to keep the colonists from expanding westward.

would strengthen New France in its rivalry against the English and the Dutch, who also realized the value of the fur trade in North America. The Dutch had already established a trading post at Fort Orange on the Hudson River and had allied themselves with the Iroquois. Dutch merchants offered trade goods, including muskets, to the Iroquois in exchange for furs. English colonies had been established in Massachusetts and farther south in Virginia. In addition, the English had established a colony in Nova Scotia.

Champlain tried to persuade the French government to recognize the importance of New France as a bulwark against the Dutch and English in North America. But he was largely unsuccessful. When he died in 1635, New France was still a small, weak colony. On all sides, it faced enemies—the Dutch, the English, and the Iroquois. Dealing with these enemies and expanding the colony became the mission of the next decades. ✳

bulwark—defense

CHAPTER THREE

The Colony Struggles

JESUIT MISSIONARIES *attempting to convert the natives are among those who settle in New France. Colonists battle the cold winters and hostile Natives, with little support from France.*

ver the next three decades after the death of Champlain, the colony of New France struggled. Pierre Boucher, a colonial official wrote:

> The Iroquois . . . hem us in so close they prevent us availing ourselves of the country's resources.... One cannot go hunting or fishing without fear of being killed or captured by those knaves: nor can one cultivate the land, still less harvest the grain, except in continual risk; for they wait in

OPPOSITE: This painting, "The Martyrdom of Three Jesuit Priests," illustrates the deaths of French missionaries Isaac Jogues, Antoine Daniel, and Jean de Brébeuf at the hands of the Iroquois. Although the three priests died in different places and years apart, the artist combined their deaths in one image in order to emphasize the impact of their deaths.

ambush on all sides. . . . A wife is always uneasy lest her husband, who left in the morning for his work, should be taken or killed and that never will she see him again.

In order to encourage settlement in New France, the Company of One Hundred Associates granted large parcels of land along the St. Lawrence River to well-to-do Frenchmen called *seigneurs*. The first seigneur in New France was Robert Giffard. A ship's doctor, Giffard came to Beauport, near Québec, in 1620.

He built a cabin along the St. Lawrence River and established an estate called a *signeurie*. A few years later he described the area where he lived, *"for that I have been there and sojourned there for five or six years continuously, and have seen and do know that the St. Lawrence River can yield fifteen thousand beavers."*

Two other seigneurs, Pierre Legardeur de Repentigny and his brother Charles Legardeur de Tilly, traveled to New France with their families and set up large estates. They were expected to attract French colonists to North America to establish farms on the estates. The two seigneurs built a gristmill to grind the wheat grown by the farmers into flour. Bread was one of the basic elements of the settlers' diet. The seigneurs also built a Catholic church on their property where the farmers could worship.

New France offered settlers, called *habitants*, many advantages. They received free land, which they could not have afforded to purchase in France. They could grow plenty of wheat in the fertile soil of Canada. Wheat was much harder to grow in France, and it was often in short supply. They were also permitted to hunt and fish on the seigneuries, unlike peasants in France who were forbidden to trespass on the estates of wealthy landowners. There was also plenty of lumber in the forests of New France, which could be cut for building shelters and to use as firewood to keep the habitants warm during the long, cold Canadian winters.

HOLIDAYS
in New France

CHRISTMAS AND EASTER were special holidays in Catholic New France. The habitants also celebrated the harvest on November 11 at their seigneur's home, after the wheat crop had been gathered and all the taxes paid to the seigneur. Another holiday was May 1, May Day, the start of spring. This was a time of festive dancing and celebration.

Still, it took the habitants enormous effort to clear the land, build a farmhouse, and establish a thriving farm. Much of the work *"had to be performed during the summer months, while dense clouds of mosquitoes and black flies made life almost unbearable for newcomers from Europe. But these insects were as nothing compared to the menace of marauding Iroquois, waiting to cut down the unwary."*

In addition to working the land, habitants were also expected to serve in the colonial militia that provided defense for the colony. Each militia unit was commanded by a captain. The militia captains also served as important local officials.

The habitants—the real pioneers of the new colony—risked their lives to settle New France. Growth was slow. By 1650, fewer than 700 habitants had settled in the colony.

RELIGIOUS GROUPS

Among the settlers who came to New France was a group of hardy Roman Catholic clergy. Catholicism was the only religious belief permitted by the government in New France. The priests dedicated themselves to converting the natives to Catholicism and guiding the spiritual lives of the French colonists. In 1635, Jesuit priests established a school for boys in Québec. By the following year, there were 20 students. They were taught by Father Charles Lalemant, the head of

clergy—people ordained to perform religious services

Jesuits—a Catholic religious order for men

the Jesuit order in New France. Over the next two decades, instruction broadened to include grammar, mathematics, French, and Catholic religious beliefs. Gradually, the Jesuits expanded the curriculum to train students in navigation so they could sail the St. Lawrence River and the Great Lakes.

Ursulines—a
Catholic religious
order for women

In 1639, three Ursuline nuns established a school for girls in Québec. Among the students at the school were the daughters of Robert Giffard, the first seigneur in New France. Some girls from native villages in the area also attended the school. The students sat on wooden benches while their teacher taught them to read. Pens and paper were made available so they could practice writing. The girls learned about the Catholic religion and were also taught homemaking skills, such as spinning and weaving.

Approximately 200 students were taught by 50 nuns at the Ursuline convent (seen in the background) in Québec. Livestock graze the fields as habitants relax in the foreground.

Marie de l'Incarnation

The leader of the Ursulines in New France was Marie de l'Incarnation, born Marie Guyart in Tours, France, in 1599. Marie was married at 17 to a prominent silk manufacturer, who died two years later. After his death, Marie wanted to become a nun, but she delayed her entry into the convent in order to raise her son, Claude. When she was 34, Marie was inspired to leave France and travel to North America. She believed her mission was to convert the Indians to Christianity. In 1639, she arrived in Québec with several other Ursuline nuns. Two years later they began the construction of an Ursuline monastery, where they educated Indian girls as well as the daughters of the French colonists. When Claude decided to become a priest, Marie wrote to her son: "My *heart received a greater consolation than any news I have had in my life. . . . Let us dwell in Jesus and see one another in him.*" We know much about the lives of the early settlers in New France from Marie's long letters to Claude telling him about her life, her love of God, and about New France.

In 1641, a group of wealthy Catholics established a new settlement at Montréal, located on the St. Lawrence River west of Québec. The primary purpose of the settlement was to serve as a center for converting Indians to Christianity. Meanwhile, Jesuit priests had been pushing westward, establishing missions among the Hurons around Lake Huron and other native peoples near Lake Michigan. One of these missions, Ste. Marie, included wooden houses for the priests, a hospital, and a church. Huron villages were located around the mission, whose priests converted hundreds of Indians to Christianity. French coureurs de bois also traveled to the Huron villages to trade for beaver and other furs. The influence of the traders and the priests built strong alliances between the Hurons and the French.

mission—a settlement founded for the purpose of converting native peoples to Christianity; also the duty or calling of one who tries to convert others

The Jesuits faced many challenges in their efforts to convert the Hurons to Christianity. The priests braved the icy cold as they traveled to the Indian villages. They had to learn the difficult Huron language in order to communicate with the Indians. They also encountered strong opposition from the medicine men, or shamans—the spiritual leaders of the Huron villages. At first, the Jesuit priests tried to convince the Hurons to give up their beliefs and to adopt Christianity. When that proved difficult, the Jesuits tried a different approach to convert the Hurons by drawing upon similarities between Huron and Catholic ideas of spirituality.

Father Isaac Jogues was a Jesuit who worked among the Indian nations. Born in France in 1607, he arrived in New France in 1636. Traveling west with other priests, Father Jogues soon reached Sault Ste. Marie. They were the first European explorers to reach this point, located between Lake Superior and Lake Huron. On his return to Québec in 1642, Jogues was captured by the Mohawks, who kept him captive for more than a year. He was finally rescued by the Dutch, who took him to Albany in New Netherland (later the English colony of New York). After his recovery, he was taken to France. Jogues returned to New France in 1644, traveling south to a lake that he named Lac St. Sacrement (called Lake George by the English). Once again, he was captured by Mohawks, who blamed him for bringing a plague among them and ruining their crops. He was stabbed repeatedly by Mohawk warriors and eventually killed with a tomahawk blow to the head on October 18, 1646. Father Jogues was canonized by the Catholic Church in 1930.

canonized—declared a saint by the Catholic Church

During the 1630s, the Jesuits began publishing *The Jesuit Relations*, an annual report of their activities. One of its goals was to attract more settlers to New France in order to increase the size of the colony. Father Paul LeJeune wrote in 1636: *"I have been asked whether by clearing the lands for cultivation and tilling them they will produce enough for the subsistence of their inhabitants. . . . I would reply in the affirmative."*

Catherine Tekakwitha

One of the Indians converted to Christianity by the Jesuits was Catherine Tekakwitha. Born in 1656, she was a member of the Mohawk nation. After her parents died of smallpox when she was only four, she was raised by her relatives. During the 1660s, when Jesuit missionaries visited the home of her uncle, she learned about Christianity. At the age of 18, Tekakwitha was converted to the Catholic faith by Father Jacques de Lamberville. Although many Mohawks were opposed to Christianity, Tekakwitha defended her religious beliefs. Finally, she was forced to leave her home and move to Kahnawake on the St. Lawrence River near Montréal. This was a community of Mohawks within New France who had been converted to Christianity. Tekakwitha was considered by the Jesuits to be a devoutly religious Catholic who *"had attained the most perfect union with God in prayer."* She died in 1680 and, late in the 20th century, became a saint of the Catholic Church.

Father Paul LeJeune was another Jesuit priest who worked among the Hurons. LeJeune wrote that the Hurons expected him to demonstrate the same powers as the shamans. The shamans treated disease and, according to the Indians, communicated with the spirit world to influence the weather and the size of Huron harvests. As Father LeJeune put it: *"our lives depend upon a single thread; and if, wherever we are in the world, we are to expect death every hour, and to be prepared for it that is particularly the case here. . . . you are the cause of droughts; if you cannot make rain, they speak of nothing less than making away with you."*

Jesuits preach to the Indians, immersing them in the rituals of Christianity.

Another Jesuit, Father Charles Garnier, added: "*The conversion of Indians takes time. The first six or seven years will appear sterile to some; and if I should say ten or twelve, I would possibly not be far from the truth.*" What added time to the Jesuits' mission was Indian resistance to the new religion and its various rituals. The Indians also believed that their own way of life was superior to that of the Europeans. As one Mic Mac elder summed it up, if France "*is a little terrestrial paradise, art thou sensible to leave it? . . . Which of these two is the wisest and happiest—he who labours without ceasing and obtains, and that with a great deal of trouble, enough to live on, or he who rests in comfort and finds all that he needs in the pleasure of hunting and fishing?*"

Another problem faced by the Jesuits was the relationship between the Hurons and the Iroquois. During the 1640s, these traditional enemies were involved in a violent conflict. Iroquois warriors invaded Huron lands, burning villages and killing and capturing thousands of men, women, and children. Some of the Hurons were fortunate enough to escape and travel to Ste. Marie, where they took refuge inside the wooden walls surrounding the mission. But the Iroquois attacks continued, destroying villages a short distance from the mission. In 1649, the Jesuits decided to leave Ste. Marie, taking Indian families with them. The power of the Hurons had been destroyed by the Iroquois.

CHAPTER FOUR

Slow Growth in New France

NEW FRANCE EXPANDS *its western borders,*
strengthening its hold on the fur trade.
Montréal becomes a center of commerce.

or the next decade, few French settlers came to
North America. France was gripped by a civil
war that finally ended in the early 1660s, when
King Louis XIV took firm control of the French govern-
ment. The king and his finance minister, Jean-Baptiste
Colbert, now began to focus their attention on developing
New France into a profitable colony. Colbert formed a new
company, called Compagnie de l'Occident (Company of the
West), to attract investors and bring more settlers to New
France. The government also appointed Alexandre de

OPPOSITE: Jean Talon (in blue), appointed intendant of New France in
1665, inspects workers in a shipbuilding yard in Québec.

Prouville, sieur de Tracy, to take charge of all French colonies in the New World.

Tracy traveled to New France with a small army of soldiers. They built several forts to protect the settlers from the Iroquois and launched a campaign against the Five Nations. The French marched into Mohawk territory, burned their villages, and destroyed their crops. This sign of French force convinced the Five Nations to sign a peace treaty in 1667. This treaty ended, at least for a while, the Iroquois threat to the French settlements and the French fur trade.

This view of Montréal shows the farm of fur trader François Desrivières in the foreground and ships sailing in the river.

Colbert appointed a new governor for New France, an accomplished military leader named Daniel de Remy, sieur de Courcelle. The duties of the governor included directing the campaigns of the colony's military and dealing with the Indian nations. A second official appointed by Colbert was the intendant Jean Talon, who arrived in New France in 1665. The intendant was in charge of financial and administrative affairs, making him just as powerful as the governor.

The intendant and governor ran New France with the assistance of the Sovereign Council, consisting of leading men in the colony. In the past, the most powerful man had been François de Laval, bishop of Québec and head of the Catholic Church in New France. Laval had been appointed bishop of Québec in 1658 by Pope Alexander VII with the support of King Louis XIV. *"We wish the Sieur de Laval . . . to be recognized by all our subjects in New France,"* the king wrote. After arriving in New France, Bishop Laval opened a Catholic seminary in Québec to train new priests. He also led a struggle to prevent the sale of alcohol to the Indians. French merchants and coureurs de bois regularly traded brandy to the Indians, hoping they would obtain more furs by making the Indians drunk. As Marie de l'Incarnation, the Ursuline nun, wrote, *"Our bishop is very zealous [in stopping the practice of selling alcohol to the Indians] for what he believes will increase the glory of God."* Laval threatened that he would excommunicate anyone convicted of selling liquor to the Indians.

Laval's influence in the government of New France gradually declined as the intendant Talon became the most powerful member of the Sovereign Council. Talon was in charge of carrying out many of Colbert's plans to make the colony of New France more financially successful. Colbert informed Talon *"that one of the greatest needs of Canada is to establish manufactures and to attract craftsmen to produce the things of daily use, for to date it has been necessary to transport to that country the cloth to clothe the people and even shoes that they might have something on their feet."*

Colbert found skilled craftsmen who were willing to travel to New France. He also sent 150 young women to Québec each year to become wives of men already living there. Many of these girls, known as *les filles du roi* ("the king's girls"), came from orphanages in France.

Colbert also sent indentured servants to the colony. These laborers were required to work on farms for three years at very little pay in return for their voyage to North America. After their service ended, they were given land to farm. In addition, soldiers assigned to the colony were given money to remain in New France after their service in the army was over.

Meanwhile, Talon was using money from the French government to finance new industries. Colonists were raising sheep and making clothing from the wool, building ships, and making shoes. But Talon admitted that it was difficult to encourage settlers to participate in these industries because of the lure of the fur trade.

Many residents in New France relied on the plentiful fish in the rivers and lakes. This 1698 painting, "Killing Sturgeon on the Shores of Lake Erie," shows two groups of fishermen. The men in the boat in the background are using guns to shoot a large sturgeon in the water, while the men on the shore are using axes to cut up a recent catch.

THE LURE OF THE WEST

For a very small investment, a settler could purchase trading goods to give to the Indians in exchange for pelts. The colonists learned from the Indians how to make birch bark canoes to carry their trade goods as they paddled waterways that took them to lands around the Great Lakes. Birch was readily available at no cost from the dense forests in New France.

In two weeks, a pair of traders traveling from Québec could reach the French trading post at Michilimackinac, located where Lake Michigan and Lake Huron meet. The 1667 peace treaty with the Iroquois made travel much safer than it had been in the past. Along the way, the coureurs de bois fed themselves by fishing in the lakes, hunting deer, and eating corn at Indian villages. Once they reached Lake Michigan, the traders could bargain with the Indians for a large cargo that could be as much as 2,500 pounds (1,135 kg) of pelts. Many of the traders learned Indian languages, lived in Indian villages, and even married Indian women.

After the summer trading season was over, the coureurs de bois returned to Montréal, where a huge fair was held each year. Merchants from Canada and France sold their goods in return for furs. The fair also attracted many Indians, who brought furs to trade with local merchants. Each year, the governor attended the fair. One onlooker described his address to the Indians:

> through an interpreter, always speaking like a father to his children, dwelling on the power and the glory of his King across the sea, impressing on them how fortunate they were to have dealings with the French. . . . This done, he distributed his presents to the chiefs; plumed hats, gay-colored coats, muskets, powder and ammunition, dresses and trinkets for [the women], toys for their children.

Talon knew that New France was dependent on the fur trade for its economy. The intendant hoped that eventually the French would establish a large trading empire across the Great Lakes and into the western regions of North America. The means to this goal were the coureurs de bois, penetrating the interior and trading with the Indians.

Relying on the fur trade, however, created problems for the colony. The opportunities for adventurous men to succeed in the fur trade caused many of them to be reluctant to undertake other kinds of work. Seigneurs complained that it was difficult to find enough farmers to grow crops on the land. Very few men became artisans or entered other manufacturing businesses. The result was the failure of Colbert's plan to turn New France into a self-sufficient colony, supplying all its own needs. Colbert had also envisioned a small but well-populated colony along the St. Lawrence River that would be easy to defend. Instead, New France stretched westward into the wilderness along the Great Lakes in a far-flung empire that was much harder to protect.

Nevertheless New France under Talon had improved greatly by the time he retired in 1672. Habitants had carved out farms in long narrow strips stretching north and south of the St. Lawrence. This long-lot arrangement provided each farm with easy access to the river, which was the most efficient means of travel between the settlements of New France. As *The Jesuit Relations* put it, "*It is pleasant to see now almost the entire extent of the shores of our River St. Lawrence settled by new colonies.*" The population was nearing 10,000. This was much larger than a decade earlier, but still small compared to the estimated 112,000 settlers who lived in the English colonies. ▨

CHAPTER FIVE

Life in 18th-Century New France

Some of New France's settlers find success, but the majority of colonists remain farmers, who make their living off the land.

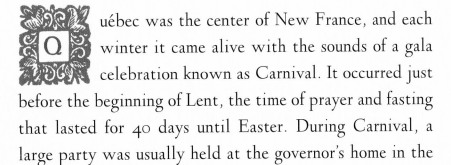

Québec was the center of New France, and each winter it came alive with the sounds of a gala celebration known as Carnival. It occurred just before the beginning of Lent, the time of prayer and fasting that lasted for 40 days until Easter. During Carnival, a large party was usually held at the governor's home in the

OPPOSITE: Many more men than women lived in New France, so newly arriving girls often had their pick of men. In this illustration, a young girl has her choice of different suitors, including a farmer, a coureur de bois, and a man of better birth, who holds a bolt of cloth likely as a gift.

The merchants had grown rich from a variety of trading ventures. Some of them, like François Havy and Jean Lefebvre, were representatives of large import-export firms with headquarters in France. They imported French cloth and lace, brandy, and furniture into New France. The merchants also sold the surplus grain grown in the colony to France's island colonies in the Caribbean. There, huge plantations grew coffee, tobacco, and sugar, which were exported to New France.

Indians and coureurs de bois mingle in a city in New France. Such meetings took place often during trading fairs.

Many merchants were also engaged in the fur trade. This trade was dominated by the merchants of Montréal and the commandants of the French military posts in Illinois Country,

the Ohio Valley, and other parts of the colony's western frontier. The merchants shipped trade goods westward to the
forts. Indians would come there to trade their furs or the com-
mandant would send trading expeditions to Indian villages.

The independent coureurs de bois had largely disap-
peared by the 18th century. They had been replaced by
voyageurs—men who worked for the trading companies,
paddling large canoes filled with piles of pelts.

Among the most successful merchants in Montréal was
Alexis Lemoine Monière. He had begun his career as a
voyageur, saved enough money to buy trade goods for his
fur business, and finally opened a trading store. In 1725, he
married Marie Josephte Couagne, a very wealthy young
woman whose father was a leading merchant in the city.
Through his father-in-law's contacts, Monière expanded
his business among other merchants in Montréal and the
military commanders at the frontier forts.

Merchants were also heavily involved in the fishing
industry along the St. Lawrence River and in Louisbourg,
located on Cape Breton Island. Established in 1719,
Louisbourg was built as a strong fortress that guarded the
entrance to the St. Lawrence, in case a British expedition
tried to attack Québec. By the mid-18th century, the town
had a population of about 2,000. As many as 200 ships lay
at anchor in the harbor at Louisbourg, carrying luxury items
from France, sugar from the Caribbean, and wheat and furs
from Québec.

THE MIDDLE CLASS

Merchants like Monière were among the upper class of New France. Below them were the colony's middle class— lawyers, doctors, small merchants, and store owners. Among the Louisbourg merchants was Jacques Rolland, who had begun his career as a clerk with a large firm in western France that traded with New France. Eventually, Rolland had moved to Louisbourg, where he first repre- sented the French merchant firm and later opened his own business. Rolland's shop was called a boutique, where he stocked colorful rolls of cotton cloth imported from Europe. He sold the material to the residents of the town to make clothing. He also carried a variety of other items, such as shoes, pipes, pencils, books, and tobacco pouches.

Rolland also financed fishing expeditions in the Atlantic. The area around Louisbourg was a rich fishing ground for cod. Jean Phelipeaux also became very successful in the cod-fishing business, employing several crews of men who fished the waters near Louisbourg. Early each morning, Charles Renaut, one of Phelipeaux's employees, gathered his crew together to venture out into the heavy seas. They trav- eled in a 30-foot boat called a shallop, which carried a sail and oars. The boat also carried barrels of herring, mackerel, and other fish, which the fishermen used to bait their nets to catch cod. On a good day, the fishermen caught several hun- dred pounds of cod. They brought the catch back to shore, split and boned the fish, and soaked it in barrels of saltwater to preserve it. Then the fish was laid out in the sun to dry before being shipped to other parts of New France or across the Atlantic Ocean to Europe.

WOMEN IN NEW FRANCE

WOMEN HAD VERY FEW RIGHTS IN NEW FRANCE DURING the 18th century. Young women were expected to obey their fathers, especially when it came to marriage. The choice of a husband was usually an arrangement between families. A girl's parents hoped that her marriage might provide them with additional land or a higher place in society. Even if a woman came from a wealthy family, any property that was given to her by her father at the time of the marriage was immediately given to her husband to manage. The main duties of upper- and middle-class women were having children and managing the household. If a husband died, however, his wife might take over his business. In 1724, Claude de Ramezey's husband, a well-to-do merchant, died in Montréal. She took over his businesses, which included a sawmill, a brickyard, and a tile manufacturing plant. Other women ran taverns or boutiques after the deaths of their husbands. However, some women were not so fortunate. Catherine Thibault, for example, had very little money after the death of her husband and was forced to send her four daughters to work as servants for other families.

Other residents of Louisbourg, Québec, and Montréal ran small shops, inns, and taverns. These were usually located on the ground floor of their houses. Pierre Morin, for example, was a stonemason who had helped construct the walls at Louisbourg. Morin was so successful that he employed a group of masons to do this work. Later he ran a small tavern. The tavern was located in the kitchen of his house, warmed by a large fireplace, where men could sit, have some food and drink, and talk after a day's work.

VERSO

In addition to business owners, the middle class also included many craftsmen. Carpenters, ropemakers, and sailmakers generally found steady employment around ports, such as Louisbourg, Montréal, and Québec. These towns also had butchers and bakers to supply food for the local residents. They sold their wares at markets twice weekly. In Québec, the government set a fixed price for bread and meat so people could

The colony of New France did not produce its own currency, so playing cards were used as a substitute for money that would be paid when funds supplied by the king arrived from France. (Each card had an amount inscribed on the back.) This practice ensured that trade would continue in the colony despite a shortage of official currency.

afford to purchase enough to feed themselves. Blacksmiths, tanners, and coopers (barrelmakers) also worked in New France. Tanners made shoes, and five of them worked in Québec, *"in view of the bad quality of the hides tanned by the country people who do not know the [tanner's] craft."* Some of these artisans were prosperous enough to hire apprentices, young boys interested in learning a trade. In return for their work, they received free room and board. Other craftsmen employed indentured servants. They received free passage to New France in return for three to five years of work.

HABITANTS

Habitants, who lived on farms outside the major towns, made up most of the population of New France. Because the colony was so far north, the growing season was usually quite short.

A Harsh Life *for the* HABITANTS

DURING THE EARLY PART OF THE 18th century, the habitants were forced to deal with a variety of natural disasters that affected their crops. Droughts occurred in 1715 and 1716. In 1720, the wheat crop was attacked and ruined by caterpillars. These disasters were followed by heavy rains in 1736. Since habitants depended on the land to feed their families and provide hay for the cows and horses, the forces of nature could play a devastating role. Most habitants tried to plan for difficult times. At the end of a good harvest, they stored extra food in the attic or the cellar of their homes. This food was often enough to bring them through the harsh, snowy winters. But in the spring, supplies were usually running low and the habitants had to hope for a warm growing season with enough rain to produce bountiful harvests to carry them through another year.

Habitants began plowing their fields in May and harvesting their wheat by late summer before the frosts arrived in early fall. While many farmers owned oxen to pull their plows, some were too poor and had to rent animals from their neighbors. After the wheat was harvested, it was threshed, using heavy sticks to separate the wheat grains from the stalks.

In addition to their fields, habitants had gardens and orchards to grow vegetables and fruit. These were usually maintained by the women, who also cooked meals for their families, made clothing, and tended the cows and pigs. Most livestock was killed each fall because it was too expensive to keep the animals inside barns and feed them during the long winters. The meat was preserved in salt to provide a steady food supply for a habitant family.

A DISTINCTIVE PEOPLE

BY THE 18TH CENTURY, THERE were written descriptions of the characteristics of the settlers who lived in New France. *"The Canadians [habitants] are naturally big, well-built, and have a robust constitution,"* wrote the intendant Gilles Hocquart in 1737. *"The rural folk all handle an axe with skill; they make the greater part of their own farming tools and implements. They also build their own houses and barns. . . . They love honors and flattery, pride themselves on their bravery, and are extremely sensitive to scorn or the slightest punishments."* And J.C.B. commented: *"The residents of Montréal call those of Québec sheep because the latter have a gentler character and are less bellicose [than those of Montréal]. In reprisal, they [Québeckers] call Montréalers wolves. . . . In general, the Canadians are forthright, kind, and hospitable . . . but they are poorly-educated."*

Habitants produced much of what they needed on their farms. Meals included meat, bread, and a variety of vegetables, such as peas, carrots, squash, onions, and cabbage. Habitants might also throw out large fishing nets along the St. Lawrence River to catch eels. The farmers used any surplus food that they produced to trade for items like pots and pans for cooking, stoves to heat their homes, tea, coffee, spices, and salt.

Unlike wealthy members of society, habitants lived in small, simple homes with a few chairs, a bed for adults, and straw mattresses on the floor for children. There were few schools in New France, and these were reserved for children of the upper class. The children of habitants did not attend school and were not taught how to read or write. As soon as they were old enough, boys usually went to work helping their fathers in the fields, while girls worked alongside their mothers in the gardens or doing chores around the house. ✖

This image, showing farms with fenced plots for livestock, dirt paths, and people fishing along the river, illustrates the simple life of habitants living in a small village near Québec.

CHAPTER SIX

New France and the British Colonies

1701–1754

THE FRENCH CLASH *with the British over control of New France and France's expansion into other parts of North America.*

 aily life in New France went on under the shadow of a long conflict between the French and British for control of North America. In 1702, war broke out once again, part of a conflict between France and England* in Europe.

OPPOSITE: Frank Earle Schoonover's painting shows voyageurs and Indians arriving at Fort Duquesne, located where the Ohio River meets the Monongahela and Allegheny Rivers. The fort played a key role in protecting New France's trade with Louisiana and Illinois Country.

*Note: In 1707, England became Great Britain, which was made up of England, Scotland, and Wales.

Philippe de Rigaud de Vaudreuil became governor of New France in 1703. During the war, he decided to launch attacks on towns in New England, including Deerfield in Massachusetts, Hampton in New Hampshire, and Wells in present-day Maine. Victory in these raids allowed the French to take prisoners, some of whom decided to stay in New France, adding to the population.

A Captive in NEW FRANCE

LATE IN FEBRUARY 1704, A SMALL ARMY OF ABOUT 200 French soldiers and their Indian allies attacked the town of Deerfield in northern Massachusetts, taking 109 men, women, and children prisoner. One of them was seven-year-old Eunice Williams. Her father, the Reverend John Williams, and her brothers and sisters were later freed, along with many of the other captives. But Eunice decided to stay in New France and live at Kahnawake, a community of Mohawks who had been converted to Christianity. Eventually, she was given an Indian name, A'ongote, and married a Mohawk, François Xavier Aroson. Although her father visited Eunice and pleaded with her to return to him, she refused, answering in the Mohawk language, *"Jaghte oghte"* ("No, she would not go"). After two years, she had forgotten how to speak English and spoke only Mohawk. She felt at home at Kahnawake, surrounded by her Indian friends. Over the next few decades, Eunice and her husband regularly visited the Williams family, but she never returned to Massachusetts permanently. She died in 1785.

privateer—pirate hired by a government to attack and rob the ships of enemy countries

Meanwhile, French ships operating out of Port Royal in eastern Acadia sailed along the coast, threatening New England towns. French privateers brought their stolen goods to Acadia, where the settlers eagerly supported the illegal trade, bartering for supplies that the French government did not provide. In 1710, the British led an expedition against Port Royal, capturing the settlement. As a result, eastern Acadia fell under the control of the British, who renamed it Nova Scotia (meaning New Scotland). The British hoped that taking over this border community would put pressure on Québec to end French and Indian raids on New England towns. Britain also hoped that the privateers' illegal activities would lessen with British control of Nova Scotia.

A view of Fort Edward, built by the British in 1750 near the border between Nova Scotia and New France. Its job was to maintain order among the Acadians living in Nova Scotia and discourage further expansion of New France in the region.

The British presence affected few of the French settlers living in Acadia. The towns of Acadia, by then home to almost 1,500 habitants, were spread over great distances with only rough paths between them. The residents were allowed to continue with their lives as before, farming along the coastline. Many habitants in Port Royal had fled when the British takeover seemed imminent. Once dependent on supplying the French fort there to make a living, they now made new lives in the far-flung villages. Although the Acadians in this area were now British subjects, they remained devoutly French, refusing to declare loyalty to Britain.

When the war finally ended in 1713, Nova Scotia remained part of the British Empire, which also took over Newfoundland and the Hudson Bay region. However, the French continued to hold Cape Breton Island. This island was north of Nova Scotia near the entrance of the St. Lawrence and guarded the approach to Québec. French fishermen used Cape Breton Island as a base for their vessels in the rich cod fishing grounds of the northern Atlantic Ocean.

THE DEFENSES
OF NEW FRANCE

While war was raging in New England, New France was strengthening its position among the Indian nations in the west. Although the French government had previously closed some of the western posts, King Louis XIV recognized that trade was essential if he wanted to maintain his North American empire and to secure native alliances.

Sieur de Cadillac arrives in Detroit in July, 1701. Cadillac is accompanied by Indians, traders, craftsmen, farmers, and soldiers who had traveled from Montréal to establish the settlement.

In 1701, the French government gave Antoine de Lamothe, sieur de Cadillac, the commander of the trading post at Michilmakinac, permission and funding to found a new trading post at Detroit. On June 4, 1701, Cadillac left Montréal with about 50 soldiers as well as some French settlers. Detroit would include a fort and a church as well as land for the new colonists to establish their farms. Cadillac planned to make as much money as possible in the fur trade. He openly traded brandy with the Indians in return for furs, which angered the Jesuits working with natives in the region. Meanwhile the merchants at Montréal complained that Cadillac was cutting off their trade. In 1710, Governor Vaudreuil finally forced Cadillac to leave Detroit and handed leadership of the fort over to

Frenchman Charles Regnault, sieur du Buisson. The king eventually appointed Cadillac governor of Louisiana, which was part of France's empire in North America.

In 1716, the king re-opened the western posts, including one at Michilimackinac, and authorized construction of new forts. In 1726, a French officer named Chabert de Joncaire was put in charge of building a new trading post on the Niagara River, which lay along the route taken by many traders between Lake Ontario and Lake Erie and places farther west. For many years, Joncaire had traded with the Senecas, who claimed the Niagara River as part of their hunting grounds. After Fort Niagara was built, the Senecas, who realized the fort had been built on their hunting grounds, asked Joncaire to tear down the building, but he refused. Without support from the British, the Senecas were powerless.

In 1731, the French began construction of Fort St. Frédéric near the southern shores of Lake Champlain. St. Frédéric was designed to protect the southern approaches to Québec. In addition, it served as a base for attacks by the French and their Indian allies against settlements in New England.

WAR BEGINS AGAIN

During the 1740s, war again raged across Europe, pitting France and Spain against Britain and its allies. The French in New France took advantage of events in Europe to launch new raids on New England towns and attack British settlements in Nova Scotia from Louisbourg. As one settler said, *"Perhaps the British would have let us alone if we had not first insulted them."* To put a stop to the raids from Louisbourg, Massachusetts governor William Shirley decided to launch an attack on the fort. Led by a Boston merchant named William Pepperell, the Massachusetts colonists gathered a force of more than 4,000 troops.

As smoke from French cannon commandeered by troops from Massachusetts clears, the French defending the post surrender to William Pepperell and the rest of his troops. A key victory for the British, the fall of Louisbourg weakened the French hold on fishing in the region and put a stop to attacks on ships traveling to and from New England.

The colonial force arrived at Louisbourg on April 28, 1745. Facing them was Chevalier Duchambon, commanding a much smaller force of about 2,000 soldiers. Within days, the Massachusetts troops had taken control of one of the French batteries at the entrance to the harbor and turned the guns against Louisbourg. *"The enemy saluted us with our own cannon,"* said one of the Louisbourg settlers, *"and made a terrific fire, smashing everything within range."* Pepperell's siege against the city ended in June when Duchambon surrendered the fortress.

siege—a military tactic in which one army surrounds another, cutting off food and supplies in order to force a surrender

War finally ended with a peace treaty signed in 1748. Britain and France agreed to return all the lands that they had conquered from each other, including territories in Europe as well as in the French and British Empires in North America and India. To counter the threat of Louisbourg, now returned to the French, the British built Halifax, a large naval base in Nova Scotia. Although peace returned to North America, it proved only a brief calm before the terrible storm of another war.

The town of Halifax, in Nova Scotia, was founded by the British in 1749 but was home to many French people who had lived in Acadia. This 1764 drawing shows a rapidly growing settlement that contained a number of churches, a large hotel, an orphanage, and several fine houses, including the governor's.

THE WAR FOR NORTH AMERICA

In the summer of 1749, Pierre Joseph Céleron de Blainville, a French army captain, led 23 canoes filled with more than 200 men along the St. Lawrence River from Montréal. He had been sent southward to the Ohio River Valley by the governor of New France, the Marquis de la Galissonière. Blainville's mission was to take control of the Ohio Valley for France.

The Ohio River Valley had enormous strategic importance for the French Empire. It lay between the settlement of Canada in the north and French settlements along the Mississippi River southward to New Orleans in Louisiana. If this area were occupied by British settlers and the Indian nations there became their allies, the French Empire could be cut in half. During the 1740s, English traders from Pennsylvania and Virginia had already penetrated the Ohio River Valley and begun living among the native peoples there. As Blainville traveled south, he saw these traders. He also discovered that many of the Indian tribes—such as the Delaware and Wyandot—seemed hostile to the French.

Blainville carried a message to the Indians from Governor Galissonière. He wrote:

> *My children, since I was at war with the English, I have learned that . . . they have taken advantage of my absence to invade lands which are not theirs, but mine; and therefore I have*

resolved to send you Monsieur de Céleron to tell you my inten-
tions, which are that I will not endure the English on my land.
Listen to me, children; mark well the word that I send you;
follow my advice, and the sky will always be calm and clear over
your villages.

The local Indian nations did not pay much attention to de Blainville. The British colonists offered excellent trade goods at low prices, and the Indians saw no reason not to trade their furs to them. Nor were the Indians particularly interested in participating in another war. From the Ohio River, the French expedition traveled into the Great Miami River in what is now Ohio. Here they encountered a Miami chief called Demoiselle, who had established a large settlement at Pickawillany two years earlier. Pickawillany had become a lucrative trading center for the British. Although Céleron de Blainville talked to Demoiselle and asked him to switch his allegiance to France, the chief refused. Disappointed, the French expedition left Pickawillany and eventually returned to Montréal with the news that French interests were being seriously jeopardized by the British.

A NEW LINE OF FORTS

The French believed that the only way to reassert their influence among the Indians was a show of force. In Paris, the French government considered an attack on the British trading post at Oswego, on the southeastern shore of Lake

Ontario. While this plan was under discussion, New France also considered establishing new posts on Lake Erie. But Louis XV refused, believing that the forts at *"Niagara and Detroit will secure . . . our communications with Louisiana."* Meanwhile, news arrived from the commander at Fort Detroit that many more Indians were trading with the British at Pickawillany. These Indians were hostile to the French at Detroit.

In response, New France finally launched a raiding party against Demoiselle and his trading village. Led by the French coureur de bois Charles Langlade, a raiding party of Ottawas and their Ojibwe allies struck Pickawillany in June 1752. Demoiselle was killed and several white traders living in the village were captured and taken to Montréal. As a result, the Miami left Pickawillany, which no longer served as a trading center in the Ohio Valley.

This was the first show of force from the French. But the new governor of New France, the Marquis de Duquesne, was plan-ning an even stronger response to the British. Duquesne wanted to build a series of forts in the Ohio Valley to impress the Indians with French strength and drive out the

Marquis de Duquesne

British. In spring 1753, on the southern shore of Lake Erie,
Governor Duquesne commissioned a new fort, called
Presqu'île. Another fort was planned south of this post
along French Creek. These forts convinced many of the
Indians in the Ohio Valley that it might be far too dan-
gerous to continue trading with the English.

A Soldier's Life
IN NEW FRANCE

AMONG THE SOLDIERS WHO LEFT FRANCE TO GO TO NORTH
America was Joseph-Charles Bonin, an artilleryman, who
reached Québec in 1751. Some soldiers, like Bonin, remained
at the capital. But many others were assigned to garrison
duty on the frontier. At Michilimackinac, for example, the
soldiers slept in the guardhouse. There was no barracks for
them, only for the commander of the post and his officers.
The average wage for a soldier was only 108 livres per year
(about $500). As the sun rose, a soldier, like Bonin, would
wake to the sound of a drum. Soldiers dressed in their uni-
forms and ate breakfast. The food, which had to be paid for
out of a soldier's wages, might consist of bread, some bacon
or beef, and dried peas. During the rest of the day, a soldier
stood guard duty for four to six hours. At noon, soldiers
stopped for lunch, followed by supper at 5 p.m. Wine was a
common drink with meals, along with brandy and beer
because water was often not safe to drink.

Meanwhile, the British were aware that they were in jeopardy of losing their position in the Ohio Valley. Governor Dinwiddie of Virginia planned to stop the French by building a British fort at the strategic point where the Ohio River, the Monongahela, and the Allegheny River came together. Much of the trade between Quebec and New Orleans traveled through this point, where Pittsburgh now stands. In mid-December 1753, Le Gardeur de Saint-Pierre, the French commander at Fort LeBoeuf, received a message from the British. It was sent by Dinwiddie and delivered by a young major in the Virginia militia named George Washington. The message warned that the French could not remain in the region. After reading the note, Le Gardeur wrote out a reply for Governor Dinwiddie: *"As to the Summons you send me to retire, I do not think myself obliged to obey it."* Once Dinwiddie received the French response, he began organizing an expedition to the forks of the Ohio River before the French could reach it. By early spring, the construction of a British fort was under way. Before the fort could be finished, however, French troops arrived and forced the British to retreat. The French immediately began constructing Fort Duquesne.

THE START OF WAR

While the French were busy building their fort at the forks of the Ohio, Major Washington was heading for the

Ohio Valley with his own small force of a few hundred men. Washington established a position at a site called Great Meadows southeast of Fort Duquesne.

By late May, a French scouting party was heading toward Great Meadows from Fort Duquesne. Led by Joseph Coulon de Villiers, sieur de Jumonville, the small advance party of about 35 men camped for the night about 5 miles (8 km) from Washington's force. Washington had received word from a friendly Indian chief called Half King that Jumonville was camped nearby. With his own force of about 40 men, including Half King, Washington set out during the night to surprise the French. He succeeded completely, attacking the French early the next morning, May 28. During the brief battle, Jumonville and some of his men were killed.

Washington took the rest of the French soldiers back to his camp at Great Meadows. Expecting that a larger force of French troops might soon arrive from Fort Duquesne, Washington and his men constructed a wooden shelter they called Fort Necessity. By the end of June, a large French force was, indeed, on its way to attack Washington's position. On July 3, this force of more than 700 men attacked Fort Necessity. From the protection of the forests, they began firing at Washington's soldiers positioned in trenches, killing or wounding many of them. Washington eventually accepted an offer by the French to surrender his position and was permitted to leave Great

Meadows and return to Virginia. Unfortunately for the British cause, Washington left among his papers Britain's plans for the Ohio Valley.

Major George Washington (in buttoned blue and red cloak)
is surrounded by a few of his men and some Indian allies at Fort Necessity
the night before the French attack. The man kneeling is blowing on a
spark ignited by a flint.

The construction of Fort Duquesne and the victory at Great Meadows meant the French now controlled the Ohio Valley. These early battles marked the beginning of the decisive conflict between Britain and France for the control of North America. 🔲

CHAPTER SEVEN

The Fall of New France

THE SEVEN YEARS' WAR *leads to changing alliances among Indian groups. An early advantage in the war does not hold for the French in the battle for North America.*

hen the war began, New France and Britain's American colonies were very different. The population of New France, not including Louisiana, was only about 55,000, compared with more than one million people living in the British colonies. New France had fewer militias than the British colonies, but they did have strong alliances with the Indian tribes around the Great Lakes and in the Ohio Valley. Although

OPPOSITE: This engraving shows the death of British General Braddock on July 9, 1755. He and his troops were approaching Fort Duquesne when they were attacked and defeated by an advance of French troops and their Indian allies. As the British and French soldiers exchange fire in the open, the Indians attack from the woods.

successful trading partners, the Indians, especially the Iroquois, had refused to entirely support the British colonies in wars against the French.

Following the first clash in the Ohio Valley, both Britain and France sent more troops to North America. The French sent a large flotilla of ships to the St. Lawrence with 3,000 soldiers on board. The British reinforced their position in North America by sending about 1,000 troops commanded by General Edward Braddock. Braddock marched west to take Fort Duquesne, but his army was ambushed by the French before it could reach the fort and Braddock was killed.

flotilla—a fleet of naval vessels

THE FORCES OF NEW FRANCE

NEW FRANCE WAS DEFENDED BY A FORCE THAT INCLUDED various types of soldiers. Among these were the Troupes de la Marine. These officers came from the leading families of New France. About 1,000 of these men served at French forts and trading posts along the frontier. In addition to these officers, men between the ages of 16 and 65 were required to serve in the militia of New France. Led by militia captains, they were organized into 165 companies that totaled about 12,000 soldiers. Since many of these men were habitants, they were not available for long campaigns, since they had to return home to harvest the wheat crop that provided bread to feed the colony. Finally, the colonial army included just over a thousand veteran troops from France.

THE CAMPAIGN OF 1756

The conflict in the Ohio Valley marked the beginning of the Seven Years' War, known in the United States as the French and Indian War. It was fought from 1754–1763, although war was not officially declared in Europe until 1756. The commander in chief of France's forces in New France was General Louis-Joseph Marquis de Montcalm.

In 1756, the French began erecting a massive stone fortress at the southern tip of Lake Champlain, called Carillon or Ticonderoga. This show of strength led the British to fear that New France was planning an attack southward from Lake Champlain and Lake George.

Montcalm, however, had assembled a force of about 3,000 men, including Indian allies, at Fort Frontenac on Lake Ontario. Montcalm met with the Indian leaders to discuss the coming campaign. They told him that their *"custom was never to fight against entrenchments or stockades, but in the forest where they understood war, and where they could find trees for cover."* Montcalm assured them that he would *"never expose [them] to the fire of artillery and musketry from the forts,"* but use them *"to watch reinforcements that might come to the enemy, and to keep a good lookout, while the French fought against the forts."*

Early in August, a flotilla of boats carried the French from Fort Frontenac across Lake Ontario. Montcalm advanced toward Fort Ontario, which was quickly evacuated by the small number of British stationed there. Montcalm moved on to Fort Oswego, which the British also surrendered. The French took the cannon and burned the fort.

During the winter months, French and Indian raiding parties attacked small villages in New York as well as settlements in Pennsylvania and Virginia. Meanwhile, small skirmishes occurred along Lake George.

VICTORY AT FORT WILLIAM HENRY

The fall of Oswego had convinced most of the Indian nations that New France was the strongest power in North America, so they decided to join Montcalm's army. In July, 1757 General Montcalm assembled the largest force ever seen in North America—approximately 7,000 troops—at Fort Ticonderoga. Among them were more than 2,000 Indian warriors from the Great Lakes. The army moved down Lake George toward Fort William Henry, which was defended by a small British force of only 2,500 men under the command of Colonel George Monro. Montcalm asked Monro to surrender, warning him, *"Once our batteries [are] in place and the cannon fired, perhaps there would not be time, nor would it be in our power to restrain the cruelties of a mob of Indians."* When Monro refused to surrender, Montcalm ordered his heavy cannon to begin firing.

Two days later, Monro agreed to surrender the fort. Fearing that the Indians might continue to attack the British,

Montcalm led his captives, including unarmed soldiers and some families who had been living at Fort William Henry, out of camp southward on August 10. Before they had traveled very far, the Indians began to cut them off. Greatly outnumbering the French, they rushed in among the British prisoners, killing more than 100. Before Montcalm could stop the massacre, others were taken captive.

Many of the Indians, upset that Montcalm had robbed them of their right to kill their enemies or to hold them as captives for ransom, left the French camp and returned to their villages. Montcalm, faced with the loss of his Indian allies and knowing that his militiamen had to bring in the wheat harvest, took his army back to Québec.

TROUBLE IN QUÉBEC

Poor summer weather in 1757 yielded a small wheat harvest—the second in two years. As a result, by winter, a famine was gripping New France. Very little bread was

A gentleman officer in New France's army

available, and riots were breaking out in Québec. Many colonists were forced to eat horse meat to survive. Even after the spring thaw opened the St. Lawrence, few supply ships were able to get past the British Navy that patrolled the North Atlantic.

Meanwhile, Britain's command of the seas allowed it to send more and more soldiers to North America. The British government, under the leadership of William Pitt, planned to use these troops to capture Louisbourg, which guarded the entrance to the St. Lawrence River, Fort Ticonderoga, which protected the approach to New France along Lake Champlain, and Fort Duquesne, the key to French defenses in the Ohio Valley.

DEFENDING NEW FRANCE

In July 1758, a British army numbering about 16,000 under the command of General James Abercromby, began to travel up Lake George toward Fort Ticonderoga, which was once again under Montcalm's command. Montcalm had only about 3,500 men—not enough to man all the guns in the fort—and not enough to withstand a siege. In spite of these handicaps, he managed to hold firm against the British attack and force a British retreat. The French had saved Fort Ticonderoga.

While Montcalm was winning this victory at Fort Ticonderoga, a large British force was laying siege to Louisbourg. The French had strengthened Louisbourg, but it would not withstand 27,000 British soldiers and sailors sent to take control of the French fortress. On July 27, the French surrendered.

British general James Wolfe leads his troops ashore at Louisbourg, which the French would eventually surrender.

In August, soon after the fall of Louisbourg, a small force of about 5,000 American colonial militia reached Lake Ontario and captured Fort Frontenac. This fort played an important role in the line of French posts in the Ohio Valley and Great Lakes region. The Americans captured a huge quantity of trading goods that the French had intended to send to their Indian allies along with supplies that were meant for other French forts.

France's loss of Fort Frontenac had a direct impact on a new British campaign against Fort Duquesne. With an army of about 7,000 troops, British General John Forbes had spent the summer building a road through Pennsylvania toward the Ohio River. The British had also been negotiating with the region's Indians, trying to turn them against the French. In October, a large gathering of chiefs traveled to Easton, Pennsylvania. There they met with the British, who agreed to build trading posts but no settlements in the Ohio Valley in return for assistance from the Indians against the French. Realizing that the tide was turning against the French, especially after the loss of Fort Frontenac had removed any French trading goods from the Ohio Valley, the Indians agreed to help the British take Fort Duquesne. The French, understanding that the fort could not be defended with only a few hundred men and no Indian allies, blew up Duquesne and retreated northward. The French were beginning to lose hope of being able to defeat the British.

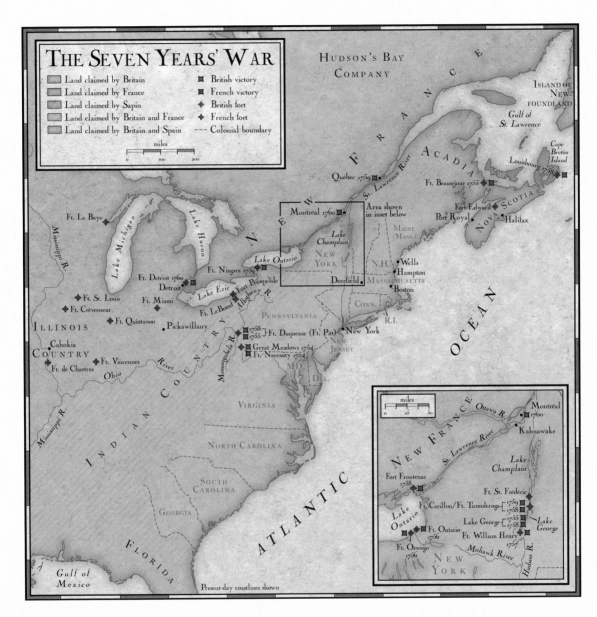

THE SEVEN YEARS' WAR

- ☐ Land claimed by Britain
- ☐ Land claimed by France
- ☐ Land claimed by Sapin
- ☐ Land claimed by Britain and France
- ☐ Land claimed by Britain and Spain
- ■ British victory
- ■ French victory
- ◆ British fort
- ◆ French fort
- --- Colonial boundary

miles
0   100   200

Humiliated by early defeats at Forts Duquesne, Oswego, and William Henry, Britain poured money, troops, and supplies into its effort to rid the North American continent of the French. With no similar aid from France, New France soon found itself on the losing end of the war. The fall of Forts Frontenac and Niagara led to the end of French control in the Ohio Valley. British victories at Louisbourg and Fort Carillon opened Québec and Montréal to attack from the east and south. By 1760, both cities were under British control. The 1763 Treaty of Paris ended the war and Frances's empire in America.

CHAPTER EIGHT

The Aftermath of War

THE ACADIANS ARE TREATED BRUTALLY *by the British.*
The siege of Québec is the decisive battle in bringing about
an end to the war.

 hile battles were being fought around the Great Lakes and in the Ohio Valley, another conflict was under way in Acadia. In 1755, the British began an attack on Fort Beauséjour, built by the French several years earlier as a defense against the British in nearby Nova Scotia and to protect their interests in the western part of Acadia. In June, British forces numbering 2,000 took over the fort. But British governor Charles Lawrence was convinced that he could never really control

OPPOSITE: French soldiers try to run for cover as British forces close in on them on the Plains of Abraham during the siege of Québec in 1759.

Acadia unless the Acadians were removed from the area. After the fall of Fort Beauséjour, Lawrence called the Acadian leaders to his headquarters. He told them that because some Acadians had fought alongside the French and had refused to take an oath of allegiance to Britain, they were *"of no use to the province . . . but rather an obstruction to the King's intentions in the settlement."*

The Acadians were ordered to hand over all their weapons to the British. Meanwhile, Lawrence began arresting Catholic priests, who were among the leaders of the Acadian communities. Lawrence also issued a secret order to the British military leaders explaining that *"It was Determined to remove all the French Inhabitants out of the Province."* He explained that ships would take the Acadians to the British colonies so that *"they may not have it in their power to return to this Province, nor to join in strengthening the French of Canada or Louisbourg."* Acadians whose families had lived in the area for generations would be forced to give up their homes and start a new life elsewhere.

Many of the Acadians were ordered to attend a meeting with British leaders. There they were immediately arrested and held until the ships arrived. Some Acadians chose to abandon their homes and escape to the woods rather than obey the British order. Françoise Leblanc later wrote that her husband, Augustin, *"remained seated for a long time [after receiving the order to meet with the British] in front of the hearth, his head in his hands. When he stood up, his face was entirely* bathed in tears. He said not a single word, but began to collect all the objects that could be carried with them" and fled. In the forests,

guerilla—a fighter who participates in surprise attacks against an enemy

the Acadians formed guerrilla bands and fought against the British, hoping to hold out until they could receive aid from Québec.

This painting shows Acadians, under British guard, waiting along the shoreline for British ships that will take them from their homeland to colonies throughout America. About 7,000 Acadians were expelled from New France between 1755 and 1762. The exile separated families and forced many into poverty and ruin.

As the Acadians were rounded up, British soldiers began burning their homes and destroying their cattle. Meanwhile, about 7,000 Acadians were loaded onto British ships for relocation to the American colonies. By winter, the ships had set sail southward, with the

Acadians packed into cramped quarters below deck. Along the way, smallpox broke out among them, and many died.

Some of the ships stopped in Boston, where about 1,000 Acadians were supposed to live. But the local government had no place to put them. Eventually, they were sent to local families who took them in and provided them with food for the winter.

Other groups of Acadians were taken to Maryland and colonies farther south. *"One group of exiles,"* according to a report, *"was forced to live for days without shelter in the snow-covered countryside, huddling together for warmth until a local minister secured housing for them."* Eventually, some of the Acadians found jobs. But often they did not earn enough to support their children. Families were torn apart as children were taken away to work as servants in the homes of strangers.

LOSING *the* CHILDREN

IN MASSACHUSETTS, MANY Acadian families protested the loss of their children. Claude Bourgeois explained that in April 1756 *"ten or twelve men came and took away from him two of his daughters...at that time employed in spinning for the family the poor remains of the flax and wool which they had saved."* When he finally managed to bring the children home, the town where he was living refused to give him *"what little support they had been providing."* Since he could not pay his rent, the owner of his home said he would send the children to other families as servants, using the money he received for rent payments.

THE SIEGE OF QUÉBEC

Up until 1758, the Five Nations had remained neutral, while the Senecas had supported the French and the Mohawks had sided with the British. But the British victories in 1758 at Louisbourg and Fort Frontenac persuaded the Iroquois to join their campaign against Fort Niagara. As a result, the British Army easily passed through the Iroquois lands in western New York. In addition, the Senecas did not inform Captain Pierre Pouchot, the commander of Fort Niagara, that British forces were approaching. As a result, Pouchot and his small force were totally surprised, and the fort surrendered in July, 1759. While this campaign was under way, a British force of about 22,000 troops arrived at the St. Lawrence River, where they began a siege of Québec.

Montcalm, with his force of 15,000 French and colonial troops, had erected strong defenses east of Québec, while the city itself bristled with cannon. West of the city, there was

Marquis de Montcalm

only a narrow coastline, with high cliffs overlooking the river. It seemed impossible that the British could land there and climb the cliffs. Montcalm reasoned that if the city could hold out until the end of September, the St. Lawrence River would begin to freeze over. Then the British would be forced to leave, and Québec would be saved.

BATTLE ON THE PLAINS OF ABRAHAM

Montcalm's plan almost worked. In September, however, the British spotted a weakness in the French defense—a small path leading up the cliffs from the narrow coastline west of the city. Montcalm had put no defenses there. As he had explained, *"we don't need to believe that the enemy has wings."* But Montcalm had miscalculated. In the dark morning hours of September 13, 1759, British forces traveled up the path and gathered on the broad Plains of Abraham, west of Québec.

General Montcalm quickly gathered a small force and rushed to battle. The British held their fire until the very last moment. Then they unleashed a terrible volley. The French line halted as men fell dead and wounded; then it collapsed and the troops fled from the field. In the short battle, Montcalm was fatally wounded, and he died the next day.

An engraving by J. and C. Bowles shows British ships positioned along the St. Lawrence off Québec and troops disembarking to follow a path up the cliffs to the Plains of Abraham, overlooking the city. Smoke from cannon and gunfire can be seen above the treetops as the French and British clash.

With the death of Montcalm, Governor Vaudreuil took charge of the French troops in Québec. He managed to lead them out of the city, before the British could enter, and take them to Montréal. The following year, French forces tried to recapture Québec, but they failed. Vaudreuil sent urgent requests to France for supplies and reinforcements, but they never arrived. In 1760, the British advanced on Montréal. Vastly outnumbered, Vaudreuil was forced to surrender the city on September 8, 1760.

Vaudreuil was the last governor of New France. By signing the Treaty of Paris in 1763, the French agreed to give up the colony to Britain. The people of what had been New France were now subjects of the British king and colonists of the British Empire. Much of New France became the British Province of Québec (see map page 102).

The Acadians who had been hiding out and awaiting assistance from the French troops finally decided to abandon their struggle and head west to resettle along the St. Lawrence. After the capture of Québec in 1759, many of the guerrilla leaders had surrendered, while others had been captured by the British.

After the war, many Acadians living in the British colonies hoped that they might go to France. Some of the Acadians paid for passage to the French colony of Saint Domingue in the Caribbean. Others went to Louisiana. Although it had been founded by France, Louisiana had been given to Spain in return for Spanish help during the war. Looking to increase the population of their new colony, the Spanish invited the Acadians to settle there. Over the next two decades, hundreds of Acadians moved to Louisiana. They adapted to the warm, humid climate, established farms, and began raising cattle and rice. Their descendants, known as Cajuns, continue to live in Louisiana today.

Cajuns—the descendants of the Acadians who settled in Louisiana after being forced out of Canada

THE FRENCH IN CANADA

During the 1760s and 1770s, British governors in Canada respected the way of life of the French settlers there.

Governor James Murray permitted the seigneurs and habitants to keep their land. The Catholic Church retained its place in Canada, and French Catholics were permitted to serve in the new Canadian government. Murray was succeeded by Governor Guy Carleton, who continued the same policies. Meanwhile, the economy of the new province became part of the vast British trading empire. Wheat grown along the St. Lawrence was shipped to Europe and to British colonies elsewhere in North America. There was also an increasing demand for timber grown in the area around Québec, which was used to build British ships.

A French farmer plows his land in the St. Lawrence valley outside the city of Québec. Québec remained a thriving city after the British takeover and many French chose to remain there.

In 1775 as the American Revolution began, an American army invaded Canada. If the Americans hoped that the French settlers would rise up against the British and help them take Québec, they were disappointed. The American attack failed. Nevertheless, three years later, France took its revenge on Britain for the loss of New France. The French king, Louis XVI, formed an alliance with the American government. By sending supplies, troops, and ships, the French helped the Americans achieve their independence.

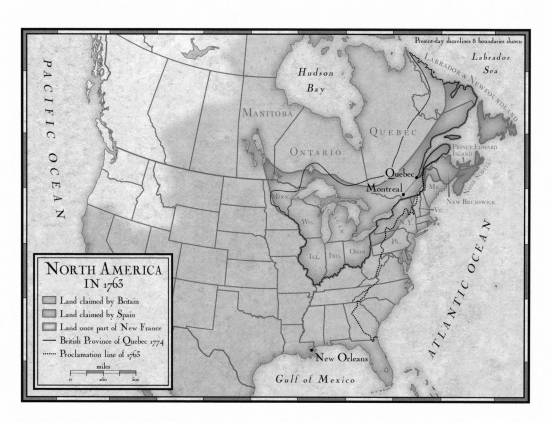

The 1763 treaty that ended the Seven Years' War left Britain and Spain as the chief landholders in North America. The present-day provinces and states that were once part of New France are shown within the blue outline.

A LASTING INFLUENCE

Although New France and the rest of France's empire on the mainland of North America ended in 1763, its influence is still very much alive not just in Canada but also in many parts of the United States. Many French people chose to stay here rather than return to France, and some of these people established communities in New England and on land that is now part of states that border the Great Lakes and the Ohio and Mississippi Rivers. Thanks to them and the explorers, missionaries, coureurs de bois, and voyageurs who preceded them, French place-names can be found from Maine to Florida and west to the Rocky Mountains. Descendants of Acadians who settled in Louisiana speak Cajun, a French dialect, and their music and food are enjoyed by millions. Throughout the country, there are businesses, organizations, and festivals that are evidence of our French heritage. Perhaps most important is the long tradition of mutual support for democratic ideals that began with the alliance that helped America win its independence. ✺

Time Line

1635 Jacques Cartier explores the
St. Lawrence River.

1608 Samuel de Champlain founds Québec, the
first permanent settlement in what becomes
New France.

1628 The Company of One Hundred Associates
sends 400 settlers to New France

1648–1649
The Hurons are defeated by the Iroquois.

1650 The population of New France approaches 700.

1665 Jean Talon becomes intendant of New France.

1672 The population of New France approaches
10,000. The French build Fort Frontenac on
Lake Ontario.

1680s New France and the Iroquois are at war.

1701 A peace treaty is signed between the Iroquois,
the French, and France's other native allies.

1702–1713
France and Britain are at war. The French
construct a trading post at Detroit.

1704 The French attack New England towns,
including Deerfield, Massachusetts.

1710 Acadia is under British control. The British
rename it Nova Scotia.

1715 The French strengthen their position by building
forts along the western edges of their territory.

1719 The French build Fortress Louisbourg on Cape
Breton Island.

1726 The French build Fort Niagara on the
Niagara River.

1731 The French build Fort St. Frédéric on
Lake Champlain.

1745 The British capture Louisbourg but return it to
France after the war.

1753 The French build forts in the Ohio Valley.

1754 The French build Fort Duquesne. The Seven
Years' War (French and Indian War) between
France and Britain begins with fighting in the
Ohio Valley.

1755 The British seize Fort Beauséjour and begin the
expulsion of the Acadians from New France.

1756 General Montcalm captures Fort Oswego on
Lake Ontario. The French build Fort
Ticonderoga on Lake Champlain.

1757 The French capture Fort William Henry on
Lake George.

1758 Montcalm defends Fort Ticonderoga. The
British again capture Louisbourg.

1759 The British capture Québec. Montcalm is killed.

1760 The British capture Montréal.

1763 New France becomes part of the British
Empire under the terms of the Treaty of Paris.

RESOURCES

BOOKS

Anderson, Fred. *The War That Made America.* New York: Viking, 2005.

Calloway, Colin. *The Scratch of a Pen: 1763 and the Transformation of North America.* New York: Oxford, 2006.

Demos, John Putnam. *The Unredeemed Captive: A Family Story from Early America.* New York: Vintage, 1995.

Faragher, John Mack. *A Great and Noble Scheme: The Tragic Story of the Expulsion of the French Acadians from their American Homeland.* New York: W. W. Norton, 2006.

Leckie, Robert. *"A Few Acres of Snow": The Saga of the French and Indian Wars.* New York: Wiley, 1999.

Moore, Christopher. *Louisbourg Portraits.* Toronto: McClelland and Stewart, 2000.

Peyser, Joseph, ed. *Letters from New France.* Urbana: University of Illinois Press, 1992.

Worth, Richard. *Voices from Colonial America: Louisiana.* Washington: National Geographic, 2005.

WEB SITES

Deerfield History Museum
http://deerfield.history.museum/dtc/

Dictionary of Canadian Biography Online
http://www.biographi.ca/

Samuel de Champlain
http://www.samueldechamplain.com

Virtual Museum of New France
http://www.civilization.ca/vmnf/vmnfe.asp

QUOTE SOURCES

CHAPTER ONE

p. 14 "set up a...furs on sticks." Riendeau, Roger. *A Brief History of Canada.* New York: Facts on File, 2000, p. 21; p. 15 "This river...trace of earth." Morrison, Samuel Eliot. *The European Discovery of America: The Northern Voyages.* New York: Oxford University Press, 1971, p. 403; p. 20 "All worked so...could scarcely see." Grant, W. L. (Editor). *Voyages of Samuel De Champlain, 1604–1618.* New York: Barnes and Noble, 1952, p.42; "all our liquors...by the pound." Grant, p. 54; p. 22 "simple, pastoral existence...a bad year." http://www.acadian-cajun.comm/origin.htm; p. 23 "to lay the...of the French." http://www.acadian-cajun.comm/origin.htm.

CHAPTER TWO

p. 28 "gave them so...happen to them." Grant, W. L. (Editor). *Voyages of Samuel De Champlain, 1604–1618.* New York: Barnes and Noble, 1952, p. 163; pp. 28–29 "I rested my...and took flight." Grant, p. 165; p. 30 "I had with...living along them." http://www.civilization.ca/vmnf/explor/brule_e2.html; "to bring them...with one another." http://www.civilization.ca/vmnf/explor/brule_e2.html.

CHAPTER THREE

pp. 35–36 "The Iroquois... see him again." Eccles, W.J. *Canada Under Louis XIV, 1663–1701.* New York: Oxford University Press, 1964, p. 3; p. 36 "for that I...fifteen thousand beavers." http://www.civilization.ca/vmnf/popul/seigneurs/seign.en.htm; p. 38 "had to be...down the unwary." Eccles, W. J. *The Canadian Frontier, 1534–1760.* Albuquerque: University of New Mexico Press, 1983, p. 38; p. 40 "My heart received...another in him." Marshall, Joyce (Editor). *Word from New France: The Selected Letters of Marie de L'Incarnation.*

Toronto: Oxford University Press, 1967, pp. 119–120, 121; p. 42 "I have been...in the affirmative." http://www.civilization.ca/vmnf/popul/seigneurs/seign.en.htm; p. 43 "had attained the...God in prayer." http://www.newadvent.org/cathen/14471a.htm; p. 44 "our lives depend...away with you." Calloway, Colin C. *The World Turned Upside Down: Indian Voices from Early America.* Boston: Bedford Books, 1994, p. 51; p. 45 "The conversion of...from the truth." http://www.civilization.ca/vmnf/popul/seigneurs/seign.en.htm; "is [France] a...hunting and fishing." Calloway, p. 51.

CHAPTER FOUR

p. 49 "We wish the...in New France." http://www.geocities.com/~hgig/belineng.htm; "Our bishop is...glory of God." http://www.geocities.com/~hgig/belineng.htm; p. 50 "that one of...on their feet." Eccles, W.J. *Canada Under Louis XIV, 1663–1701.* New York: Oxford University Press, 1964, p. 46; p. 52 "through an interpreter...for their children." Eccles, p. 63; p. 53 "It is pleasant...by new colonies." Eccles, W. J. *The Canadian Frontier, 1534–1760.* Albuquerque: University of New Mexico Press, 1983, p. 71.

CHAPTER FIVE

p. 56 "This position put...without any fear," Moogk, Peter. *La Nouvelle France.* East Lansing, Michigan: Michigan State University Press, 2000, p. 130; p. 63 "in view of...the [tanner's] craft." Moogk, p. 78; p. 64 "The Canadians [habitants]...the slightest punishments." Moogk, p. 78; "The residents of...are poorly-educated." Moogk, p. 78.

CHAPTER SIX

p. 68 "Jaghte oghte." Demos, John. *The Unredeemed Captive.* New York: Knopf, 1994, p. 107; p. 73 "Perhaps the British. . . insulted them." Leckie, Robert. *"A Few Acres of Snow": The Saga of the French and Indian Wars.* New York: Wiley, 2000, p. 248; p. 74 "The enemy saluted...everything within range." Leckie, p. 230; pp. 75–76 "My children since I...over your villages." Parkman, Francis. *Montcalm and Wolfe, Vol. I.* Boston: Little, Brown & Company, 1902, p. 42; p. 77 "Niagara and Detroit...communications with Louisiana." Parkman, Francis. *Montcalm and Wolfe, Volume I.* Boston: Little, Brown, 1902, p.85; p. 79 "As to the...to obey it." http://www.cmhg.gc.ca/cmh/en/page_189.asp.

CHAPTER SEVEN

p. 85 "custom was never...against the forts." Leckie, Robert. *"A Few Acres of Snow": The Saga of the French and Indian Wars.* New York: Wiley, 2000, p. 102; p. 86 "Once our batteries...mob of Indians." Leckie, p. 123.

CHAPTER EIGHT

p. 94 "of no use...in the settlement." Faragher, John Mack. *A Greath and Noble Scheme: The Tragic Story of the Expulsion of the French Acadians from Their American Homeland.* New York: Norton, 2005, p.316; "It was Determined...of the Province." Leckie, p. 335; "they may not...Canada or Louisbourg." Leckie, p. 335; pp. 94–95 "remained seated for...carried with them." Leckie, p. 343; p. 96 "One group of...housing for them." Faragher, p.375; "ten or twelve...they had saved." Faragher, p. 379; "what little support...had been providing." Faragher, p. 379; "we don't need...enemy has wings." Leckie, Robert. *"A Few Acres of Snow": the Saga of the French and Indian Wars.* New York: Wiley, 2000, p. 201.

INDEX

ABOUT THE AUTHOR AND CONSULTANT

RICHARD WORTH has written several biographies and histories for middle graders, including *Thomas Nast, Henry VIII, Stanley and Livingston, Ponce de Leon, Pizarro, Westward Expansion and Manifest Destiny, Women in Combat,* and *The Spanish Inquisition.* He is also the author of *Voices from Colonial America: Louisiana.* He lives in Fairfield, Connecticut.

JOSÉ ANTÓNIO BRANDÃO is an associate professor of history at Western Michigan University. He earned his Ph.D from York University in Toronto, Ontario, in 1994. He teaches courses on the history of early North America and on the history and culture of native peoples to about 1783. He has published numerous articles, chapters, and books. His most recent publications include *Nation Iroquois: A Seventeenth Century Ethnography of the Iroquois* and, as co-author, *Canada: My Country, Our History Since 1914.* He lives in Kalamazoo, Michigan.

ILLUSTRATION CREDITS

1685

BAFFI
BAY

ARCTI

NEW NORTH
WALES

NEW SOUTH
WALES

HU

Tract of Land
full of Wild Bulls

LAKE SUPERIOR

SEA OF CALIFORNIA

NEW
MEXICO

New Mexico

MEXICO

NEW ALBION

SEA OF

NEW BISCAIA

ZACATECA

THE GOLF or
BAY OF
MEXICO

SEA

OF

NEW SPAIN

YUCATAN

HONDRAS